Positive Thinking

Alter Your Thought Process In A Step By Step Fashion To Improve Problem Solving, Make More Insightful Decisions, And Produce Superior Outcomes

(Shift Your Mind-Set From Negative To Positive And Cultivate A Lifelong Optimism)

Thorsten Kremer

TABLE OF CONTENT

Is Cognitive Behavior Therapy Effective? 3

Listen To Positive Persons And Settlements Around You 15

Positivity And The Importance Of The Present 36

Establishing Goals 61

Strength Of Cleaning Up Your Social Media 77

Getting Rid Of Fear And Doubt 90

A Chancer To Success Versus Conscious Thoughts 115

Is Cognitive Behavior Therapy Effective?

Yes, it does, and we'll explain how in the response. Though the origins of cognitive behavioral therapy date back to the 1950s and 60s, the technique has evolved to the point where it is now widely used to assist individuals worldwide in reclaiming their lives as adults.

If one wishes to learn about the origins of mindfulness, one must go back thousands of years to the Buddhist and Hindu traditions. Because they believed that accepting what was happening and staying in the present moment was crucial for calming our racing minds, mindfulness developed during that time. This demonstrates how long-standing the fundamentals of cognitive behavioral therapy have been. The only distinction is that modern cognitive behavioral therapy is structured, increasing the likelihood that you will think positively and act healthily.

An area of your brain called the limbic system is responsible for processing primal survival instincts, including the instinct to fear. This system comprises several areas, including the hippocampus, which is responsible for replaying traumatic memories, and the amygdala, which handles emotion processing.

Brain scan investigations have shown that individuals with phobias have hyperactivity in these two brain regions. Nevertheless, these areas revert to normal following Cognitive Behavioural Therapy participation.

According to another research, cognitive behavioral therapy is higher-order thinking. Cognitive Behavioural Therapy can alter our "emotional brain," or our instincts, and our "logical brain," or our thoughts.

Researchers have found that the alterations in the brain that occur in patients receiving Cognitive Behavioural Therapy are comparable to those of those receiving medication. Thus, drugs and psychotherapies may affect the brain in the same way.

However, employing cognitive behavioral therapy has a benefit over taking medicine. Cognitive Behavioral Therapy has fewer negative effects when weighed against the adverse effects of medications. Compared to those taking medicine, many patients receiving cognitive behavioral therapy frequently see long-lasting results after a brief time.

Studies involving individuals with social anxiety disorder and post-traumatic stress disorder (PTSD) have been conducted. The findings indicate that these patients typically improve following a few sessions of cognitive behavioral therapy, and their improvements typically last even if they decide to discontinue treatment. This is because they already have the resources to alter their attitudes and actions.

While cognitive behavioral therapy is fantastic, not everyone will benefit. In general, this therapy aids in your problem-solving with ongoing concerns. Therefore, it is essential to combine Cognitive Behavioural Therapy with other longer-term forms of therapy if it is complex and dates back to your early years. This is because the sessions in Cognitive Behavioural Therapy are restricted, and the issues you face could take longer to resolve.

To be effective in Cognitive Behavioural Therapy, you must be prepared to devote yourself to the process and complete the assigned "homework." Furthermore, you must be willing to face your doubts and fears, which is never an easy task. People react differently to cognitive behavioral therapy, and some gain more from it than others.

Chapter 5: Developing a Thankful Attitude: The Secret to Gratitude

Gratitude is a strong emotion that can significantly improve our general happiness and well-being. We can reap many advantages by developing an attitude of appreciation, from enhanced relationships to better mental health. We will discuss the value of gratitude in this chapter and offer doable strategies for cultivating a more appreciative outlook.

Recognize the Significance of Being Thankful: Understanding the importance of thankfulness in our lives is a prerequisite for embracing it. Gratitude is connected to improved emotional well-being, happiness, and mental health. Recognizing the positive aspects of our existence promotes optimism and helps us keep a balanced perspective.

Maintain a Thank-You Notepad: Maintaining a daily gratitude notebook, where you record your blessings, is useful for developing thankfulness. This exercise turns your attention from negative to positive thoughts and invites you to count your blessings. This has the potential to gradually rewire your brain to become more sensitive to the good things in life.

Engage in Mindful Reflection: Set aside some time every day to consider the people, things, and facets of your life for which you are thankful. Increase your appreciation for the blessings in your life by purposefully concentrating on gratitude.

Show Your Thankfulness to Others: Showing your thankfulness to those in your immediate vicinity is an additional strategy for developing an attitude of gratitude. This can be accomplished with small acts of kindness like offering sincere praise, writing a meaningful note, or saying "thank you." This improves the quality of your relationships and your sense of thankfulness.

Establish Rituals of Gratitude: Make thankfulness a part of your everyday routine by creating rituals that encourage it. For instance, you may list three things you are thankful for at the beginning or consider your day's highlights at the end. These routines can support you in cultivating a more upbeat attitude in life and helping you keep up a regular practice of appreciation.

Concentrate on the Good: When faced with difficulties or disappointments, look for the bright side or the lessons that can be drawn from the circumstance. Even in trying situations, keeping your attention on the good things in life helps foster thankfulness and keep you thinking more positively.

Be in the company of thankful people: Your attempts to develop an appreciative mindset can be strengthened, and a positive support system can be established by surrounding oneself with positive people who also practice thankfulness.

Gratitude is a strong tool that can be used to improve our mental, emotional, and social well-being. We can experience the positive effects of optimism by cultivating a thankful mentality and regularly practicing gratitude.

Hope

Optimism has a big impact on positive thinking. Here are a few ways that optimism modifies our viewpoint:

Positive Outlook: Optimism cultivates a positive outlook on life. People who think positively usually expect good things to happen and think opportunities and possibilities are ahead. This optimistic perspective encourages positive thinking by influencing their thoughts, feelings, and overall perspective.

Resilience: Optimism and resilience go hand in hand. Because setbacks are temporary, they view them as opportunities for growth and education. Their persistence allows them to maintain their optimism in the face of adversity.

Problem-Solving: Optimistic people address problems head-on, concentrating on finding solutions. They believe that challenges can be conquered; thus, they actively search for answers to issues. This approach to problem-solving promotes hopeful thinking by placing a significant emphasis on possibilities and locating practical solutions.

Self-Belief and Confidence: Optimistic people typically have high self-assurance and confidence in themselves. They believe in their abilities, resources, and potential for success. This assurance inspires optimism, empowering individuals to pursue their goals and make informed choices.

Positive Interpretation: Optimistic People see the good in people and circumstances. They search for opportunities for improvement, lessons to be learned, and bright spots. This constructive reading strengthens positive thinking by reorienting the emphasis from negativity to resilience and optimism.

Positive Relationships: Relationships are positively impacted by optimism. Relationships with others are generally healthier and happier for optimistic thinkers. They approach relationships with kindness, openness, and trust, which encourages positive thinking inside them and fosters a supportive atmosphere.

Better Mental and Physical Health: Optimism has been linked to improved mental and physical health. Lives, and they also suffer from reduced levels of stress, worry, and depression. This enhanced well-being feeds on optimistic thoughts and starts an optimistic domino effect.

Optimism is the fuel that drives motivation and the achievement of goals. Positive thinkers are driven to act and persist in the pursuit of their objectives because they have faith that their efforts will yield favorable results. This drive upholds concentration, willpower, and optimism by seeing the potential in everything.

People's ability to think positively can be greatly improved by practicing optimism. Strategies that can promote optimism and assist positive thinking include:

Talking to oneself positively.

Being grateful.

Reframing negative ideas.

Surrounding oneself with positive influences.

Emphasizing one's accomplishments and abilities.

Adopting a positive outlook empowers people to face life with optimism, fortitude, and faith in the efficacy of positivity.

Listen To Positive Persons And Settlements Around You

Greetings on the third day of the 14-day course on positive thinking!

We'll examine the effects of our social environment on our mental health and state of mind. Our capacity to uphold a positive perspective and foster a support network can be greatly enhanced by surrounding ourselves with good influences.

Think for a moment about the individuals you frequently engage with. Do they usually have an upbeat and cheerful attitude, or do they usually have a negative and draining attitude? It's critical to assess how these interactions affect your perspective. Positive people may uplift, support, and encourage others when things are tough.

Think about the attributes you look for in a fulfilling relationship. Are there any particular people that exemplify these traits? List the individuals in your life who inspire and encourage you. These people could be mentors, friends, relatives, or even members of internet groups. Attempt to spend more time with them, reach out to them, and express your gratitude.

Don't give up if you discover that the people in your social group are negative. Look for new groups or communities that share your goals and values. Join clubs or go to events to network with like-minded people. You may foster and support your positive thinking journey by surrounding yourself with positive people.

Apart from individuals, the tangible surroundings we occupy also have a big impact on our mentality. Think of the locations you often visit, like your house, place of employment, or favorite hangouts. Do these areas make you feel happy and positive? If not, it could be time for some adjustments.

Spend some time today, making your physical surroundings uplifting and motivating. To create a feeling of peace and order, tidy up and arrange your surroundings. Keep things, sayings, or pictures that inspire and motivate you all around you. Aspirational and uplifting aspects should be incorporated into your space. Digital locations, in addition to physical ones, have a significant influence on our attitude. Analyze your media consumption and internet interactions. Are you interacting with and following accounts that share content that encourages growth and positivity? Or are you surrounded by negative people, making comparisons, and too dramatic?

Make thoughtful selections for your digital environments by deleting depressing accounts and looking for sources of knowledge, inspiration, and drive. Interact with material that supports your path toward positive thinking. Building a resilient and upbeat mindset is facilitated by surrounding yourself with good people, both online and off.

As Day 3 draws close, consider the supportive individuals and surroundings you have noted. Recognize the influence they have on your outlook and overall health. As we move closer to positive thinking, we'll examine the effectiveness of concentrating on solutions rather than problems tomorrow. Continue to appreciate the good things in your life, and never forget that you can affect the people around you.

DAY 4: PURPOSE SOLUTIONS FIRST

Greetings on Day 4 of the 14-day course on optimistic thinking!

We'll look at the benefits of changing our attention from issues to solutions today. We frequently think about our difficulties and problems, which might result in a pessimistic outlook. By intentionally focusing on the answers, we give ourselves the ability to overcome obstacles and develop a positive mindset.

Think briefly about a challenge or issue you are now dealing with. Acknowledging its existence in your life, put it in writing. Next, change your perspective by concentrating on possible fixes. Raise your mind to a creative and broad state of thought by asking yourself, "What are three possible solutions to this problem?" No matter how absurd they sound, jot down any ideas that occur to you.

Let's now investigate the potential of each answer. Spend some time imagining the advantages and good effects that each possible solution you found might bring. Permit yourself to visualize the situation in great detail. What would it feel like to triumph over the obstacle? In what ways might your life be altered? Take in all of the good feelings connected to these imagined solutions.

Recall that concentrating on solutions allows you to take the initiative to address problems. It changes your vibe from one of hopelessness or immobility to one of acceptance and opportunity. You position yourself for advancement and development when you focus your ideas and actions on finding answers.

When faced with an obstacle or issue during the day, deliberately adopt a solution-focused mindset. Take a moment to ask yourself, "What is a potential solution here?" as an alternative to focusing on the issue. Push yourself to use your imagination and approach the situation with a problem-solving perspective. Jot down any thoughts or activities that occur to you.

Additionally, surround yourself with positive people who promote a solution-focused attitude. Talk about ideas and get guidance from people who approach problem-solving constructively and positively. You strengthen your problem-solving acuity by surrounding yourself with others who are solution-oriented.

Never forget that every obstacle offers a chance for development and education. Accept that issues are merely obstacles to growth and solutions for yourself. Remind yourself that you can overcome challenges by coming up with solutions when you face them.

Honor your accomplishments in turning your attention to solutions. Recognize the advantages this change in perspective provides for your general well-being. As we move closer to positive thinking, tomorrow, we will examine the practice of daily positive affirmations and visualization. Continue believing in the power of solutions and your ability to overcome obstacles with fortitude and hope.

Why Is It Important To Try To Think Positively?

Positive offers the following significant advantages:

✓ It helps you achieve what you want: An old proverb goes, "What the mind can conceive, it can achieve." When you have a strong desire for something and firmly believe you can achieve it, it becomes "easier" to get it. You won't view obstacles as roadblocks but rather as opportunities to move closer to your objective, and you'll be less likely to give up in the middle of things.

✓ It improves your mood: Considering the worst-case scenario in any given circumstance is never pleasant. Even in the greatest situations, pessimists can never be content because they always expect the worst. They live on the edge. Conversely, an optimist knows that a good break is on the way. Thus, they can feel happy even in trying circumstances and are more at ease.

✣ It enhances performance: You are less likely to struggle with tasks when speaking positively. Being positive helps you see the difficult things you can improve at with effort, which keeps you from giving up and giving up on things.

✉ It enhances your general health: Martin Seligman and colleagues from Dartmouth University studied individuals between the ages of 25 and 65 to determine how their optimism and pessimism impacted their physical health. The study results showed that pessimists' health declined with age.

✣ It Reduces Depressive Episodes: People who blame themselves for their failures are more prone to experience chronic stress, which in turn can cause sadness. Optimists view failure as a teaching opportunity and move on from it, believing that good things will come of it in the future.

✉ Reduces mortality from cardiovascular diseases: A Mayo Clinic study discovered that optimists typically have a lower incidence of cardiovascular disease.

✓ Better stress management techniques: An optimist is more likely to handle stress successfully since they don't focus on the negative aspects of the situation, make the most of the difficult ones, and hold out hope for better times. Concentrating on "how bad the situation is" makes you feel more stressed because it prevents you from imagining a brighter future.

At this point in the book, if you have been a negative thinker, you should have realized that changing your mindset is necessary to live a happy life and eventually stop worrying so much about how difficult life is.

In the next part, we'll look at ways to adopt a positive outlook on life and positively impact it.

Section 2: Changing Your Thought Process to Become an Upbeat Thinker

Here's what you should do to turn your mind into a bio-computer that craves positivity:

First, Recalibrate Your Brain

Retaining your brain to think positively is possible, but it is not simple. It will take time and constant practice to achieve this. It is really important to be persistent and patient.

Our negativity-biased minds have an advantage when combating negative thinking since the mind is hardwired to focus more on bad experiences.

Since our ancestors were hunters and gatherers, our brains have evolved to recognize risks, and as a result, our self-protective feature monitors our brains for threats. This is because humans are naturally negative. This could help to explain why the negative has greater influence than the good, making it a superpower. Furthermore, it is simpler to recall the negative information than the positive.

We can all escape the negative feedback cycle and rewire our brains to think positively, regardless of our "negative wiring." We can accomplish this by altering the way we communicate with ourselves.

Your brain's neurons link with one another and exchange information through synapses. These relationships shift with each new thing you learn. Each time you practice anything new, your brain circuits are reactivated, improving synaptic efficiency and strengthening and facilitating connections' reactivation.

This means that certain skills, like driving, need less mental effort over time when you practice them frequently. You won't have to push yourself as hard to complete these tasks. The brain's innate predisposition to look for negatives can be overcome by practicing awareness and looking for the bad things in life. According to Shawn Anchor, who created the positive Tetris effect that served as the impetus for the aforementioned "brain re-tuning" procedure.

The question yet stands: just how can one reprogram one's mind to begin thinking positively again? Next, we will discover that.

Chapter Four: Put an End to Negativity

Move on.

You got into problems in the first place because you were fixated on the bad. Moving away from the things that reinforce the negative is one approach to temporarily end the negativity.

Do you work a job where you must always be prepared and always have your phone or beeper? Next, set aside some time every day to eliminate it. Switch it off. Avoid it at all costs.

Do you occasionally find that, despite being a useful tool, the internet exposes you to items that could confirm your negative thoughts? (email, news bulletins) Switch it off. Don't simply log off. Don't merely stroll around. Switch it off.

Is the negative vibe around you in your home life wearing you out and depleting all of your vitality? Step outside, even if it's just temporarily. If you have any, spend more time with upbeat and supportive friends and family. If not, give yourself more time.

Step outside. Move to an area with grass, trees, and wildlife. You can tell that these organisms do not function under stress. The grass doesn't panic in strong winds, and trees don't rush. If you spend more time in nature, you may pick up all the knowledge you need to think positively. While some people may believe otherwise, I'm not saying the trees will speak to you. However, that doesn't imply you can't gain knowledge from them.

Take Stock of Yourself

You've undoubtedly heard the phrase "head in the clouds." Your mind is the clouds; it's not in the clouds; that's the only issue. You aren't here while you're dozing off to the realm of anxiety and terrifying nightmares. Here, firmly planted on the Earth, are your feet. Either seated or standing, your body is here. Nevertheless, you are not here because, like most people, you strongly identify with your thinking. You are not in a pleasant area at all where you are.

You must make the time to quiet your mind and take in your surroundings to anchor yourself. What's going on right now? The visit with the doctor on Tuesday next week? That will occur in the future; it is not happening right now. Is there anything you need to do to guarantee a successful appointment? If so, carry it out. Let the appointment go if the answer is no. You're not present. This is where you are. Breathe, read these words, allow your heart to beat, your eyes to see, your ears to hear, and your nose to smell. Come back to Earth; you are missing out on a great time because you are preoccupied with potential negative experiences in the future.

Establish and Achieve Your Goals

Simply proving the notions incorrect is an excellent method to silence negative thoughts. Sometimes, negativity suggests that you are incapable of achieving your goals. So, going out and accomplishing it is the best way to turn off negativity. Or at least take some action. Until you reach the next checkpoint on your run, negativity will keep shouting that you won't make it. After that, it will select a different checkpoint to doubt and shout at you for failing to complete it. Up to that point. That will continue for a short period, but not for very long. You'll be less likely to accept that small voice when it makes another claim the more you refute the negative inclination in your thoughts.

You credit the negative thoughts if you allow them to cause failures or a lack of effort. Essentially, you're instructing your brain to trust them the next time. However, your brain becomes naturally more skeptical of such negative thoughts in the future when you overcome the negative thoughts and succeed despite them.

Go About

Exercise is not only a useful tool for creating and achieving objectives; exercising itself can also help reduce the tendency to think negatively. Initially, aerobic activity has the potential to reduce the size of the amygdala, which is the brain region accountable for the majority of anxiety and depression symptoms. This implies that, unlike earlier, when it might have been more overwhelming, you can block off the negative more successfully.

Second, engaging in any form of exercise promotes the release of feel-good hormones like norepinephrine and serotonin, which improve your capacity to handle stress. Additionally, it releases "endorphins," which are molecules that physically make you feel happy and fulfilled. Yes, physical activity truly can make you joyful.

Discover Your Gratitude

Dwelling on what is or could be wrong is known as negative thinking, and it flourishes when everything that is or could be right is not acknowledged. Finding the things you are grateful for instead of the things you are furious about is one of the finest ways to instantly change how you see the world, yourself, and your life.

This does not imply that you should forgo the necessities in your life or refrain from making the necessary changes. No. However, you are causing an imbalance by concentrating on these things. An imbalance that leads your brain to believe that you have always had a bad life. Furthermore, it is untrue. Whatever your identity, you can always find something for which to be thankful. And suddenly, your life appears a little more balanced because you can identify them.

There is a lot of positive in it, so it's not all negative hype. You will probably find more good in the world if you acknowledge the good that has already occurred. However, if you don't see the positive, you might look it in the face and fail to see it when looking for you.

Steer clear of the negative.

This does not imply a lack of awareness or disregard for the bad. However, it is sufficient to realize that the world can occasionally be a terrifying and horrible place. You don't need to tell yourself this every second of the day. Actually, given the state of the world, it is more likely that you will forget the good than the bad. That is what needs confirmation.

Therefore, attempt to do the opposite rather than surround yourself with people and activities that highlight all that is wrong with the world, the nation, the state, the city, or possibly even you. Seek out those who can see the good in things and make an effort to spend as much time as possible with them. Although we have a lot of internal control over our attitude, we are nonetheless influenced by the people and things we spend the most time thinking about or spending time with. Make an effort to think positively, and your mind will oblige.

Seek the Light

We might read a thousand papers from a hundred institutions discussing likelihoods, statistics, and percentages. Still, the truth is that you can manipulate a study to produce any conclusion you want. That is if they are carried out improperly.

The study's principal investigator is more likely to make the kinds of scientific errors that lead to precisely the results they were hoping for if they strongly desire a particular outcome. That's a lot like negativity.

You will only ever see the unlucky, the sick, the homeless, and the impoverished when you look at the world in that light. The birds' sweet chirping and the tidy appearance of the tree leaves before rain will be unfamiliar to you. Those who reject pessimistic notions about society will also.

Try focusing on the positive instead. Attempt to locate the light since it exists. You are aware of the existence of the dark. You probably already received a thorough education and have studied it extensively, so you don't need to look for it. What has escaped you are the good things about you, your friends, your family, and the world. How about you attempt to locate them? Why don't you search for the light, find it, and discover why those who could annoy you with their constant optimism are so content?

Positivity And The Importance Of The Present

Being in the now allows you to recognize and value life's blessings, making you feel content and joyful. You become optimistic and inevitably notice the good things when you focus on the here and now. Thus, your thoughts are likewise positive when you concentrate on the positive aspects of life.

You start using this optimism to attract more good things into your life, which makes you feel better overall. I want to stress again that adopting a positive outlook does not equate to avoiding issues. It entails viewing the issue from an impartial standpoint. The likelihood of coming up with a sound solution for the current issues is increased by this objectivity.

I acknowledge that it can be challenging to live in the moment when our thoughts are preoccupied with tasks that need to get done later on or with the potential consequences of past deeds. But, we may use the power of "now" more often than we currently do. To accomplish this, concentrate on the good aspects of your current situation.

Here's how to begin attempting to live in the present moment. Right now, what are you doing? You are reading this book. Pay attention to the reading's positive aspects. As an illustration:

You are literate if you read this book; many others cannot and will never be able to read or enjoy a book.

The fact that you are reading this book indicates that you have the means to purchase it; many worldwide struggle to eat one square meal a day, let alone afford a book.

If you are reading this book, it indicates that you are seeking methods to improve your life. Many people may have the resources to read and purchase books but are never motivated to improve themselves. They believe that life is limited to what they can currently perceive. On the other hand, you are aware that life is about more than consuming food and liquids, resting, and laboring. You are lucky!

I hope you now understand how to notice the positive aspects of the present moment by keeping your attention on the here and now. During the day, set aside some time to concentrate and take stock of your circumstances. Make a list of the advantages you perceive from the circumstances. And you will hold the power of the present. Recall to incorporate the good things in life with the here and now. Omit the bad things.

As you look deeply within yourself, you'll notice many things for which you are thankful and fewer for which you have grievances. Your life will become more joyful and meaningful as a result of this.

These easy exercises will help you develop a deep-rooted habit of positive thinking in your mind. When you're thinking only good things, your mind will be more open to doing the following:

Reaching your objectives in life

living the life that you choose to live

Getting what you desire out of life

Furthermore, someone who thinks positively is significantly more productive than someone who obsesses about their problems. Here's how to do it:

Helping the positive thinker is something that other people love to do. By doing so, you can use other people's skills and abilities. Nobody wants to be around bitter, enraged, or unhappy people. Conversely, everyone enjoys working with cheerful, smiling people. It increases your output.

Saves time by avoiding time wasted on complaints: Time is squandered needlessly when you complain. Rather, wouldn't it increase productivity if you utilized that time to solve a problem?

Boosts energy levels: Thinking positively and surrounding yourself with positive people makes you feel more upbeat and productive. This is because you can do more when you avoid thinking negative and gloomy things.

Uplifts the team as a whole because positivity and negativity are contagious. Your emotions affect your team; if you are unhappy, your team is affected by that as well. Therefore, share joy and positivity to keep your team upbeat and prepared to face work-related obstacles. This mindset is also beneficial to a family.

Resolve issues. Avoid creating problems: Consider how often you have been able to laugh off an issue and make it go away. Of course, the issue remained; the room's animosity dissipated when everyone laughed at your joke. Everyone had a positive mindset as a result, and solutions emerged. Conversely, a pessimistic mindset can magnify a small issue!

Positive thinking is a simple attitude to adopt. You will find it impossible to be negative when you have tried to understand and perfect it! All you need to do is trust your subconscious mind and inner strengths and put them to work for you.

Section Three

Protect Your Thoughts, Since They Shape Your Life

Guard your psyche, and remain alert to those individuals and external circumstances that want to undermine or rob you of your tranquility, delight, and contentment. Even if they might not be aware of it, spending as little time as possible with certain individuals or events is better. Consider the people that bring you down, and try to avoid or spend as little time as possible with them because they undermine your self-worth. Don't allow others to take advantage of you or make you feel like you always need to do things to appease them. Nobody uses you as a doormat. Instead of doing what you feel obligated to do, do the things for others that make YOU happy. There are TOXIC buddies, which is the issue at hand. These are the people who either USE you or whose lousy, negative mindsets rub off on you. Any relationship should be a fifty-fifty give and take; if you find yourself giving everything, it's time to call it quits and find someone else. Of course, there may be occasions when friends require your help, but if this occurs frequently enough to sap you, the friendship is not worthwhile. Toxic friends make you feel self-conscious. Nobody has the right to devalue you in the way they do.

Think only positive, confident ideas to help you feel good about yourself. You will be happier, more successful, and healthier if your mind is in good shape. Volunteering is one activity that can improve your self-worth and general well-being; you can choose how this manifests itself. Make a cake for your lonely neighbor and give it to her without expecting anything. You must realize that you are a self-sufficient individual who does not require the endorsement of others. Donate without placing a value on it. Volunteer at the neighborhood dog shelter or just provide a helping hand because it makes you happy. That's when you'll see the difference between giving out of obligation and giving because it brings delight. This will make you feel happy, leading to a healthy mentality, which will help you accomplish your personal goals without questioning your abilities. You can think clearly and make wiser decisions when in a good mood.

Tell yourself immediately that you won't let your ideas rule you, allow yourself to let go, and shift your attention to moving on with your life as soon as you catch yourself overly preoccupied with your thoughts. Replace those unhealthy ideas with constructive ones.

It's essential to set time limits for social media use. Our daily chores already keep our minds somewhat occupied. Without realizing it, you are causing mental turbulence when you focus on images of the newest trends, what color shirt to buy, and how you compare to ideal models. There is never a moment of calm in your head. This may cause you to feel anxious and overburdened, but it may also cause you to feel self-conscious. Some people become lost in the world's expectations of their lives and lose sight of who they are. There is no such thing as social media. The reality is that those aspiring celebrities are concealed behind that account, which most likely has many phony followers. You shouldn't follow those who appear to have it all because they don't. The whole point of social media is to flaunt your life's success, prosperity, happiness, and popularity to the world. These are typically the ones who lead sad lives. The attractive women with flawless pictures are not real; they have spent hours retouching and applying excessive cosmetics. Some have even taken extreme measures, such as undergoing plastic surgery, to flaunt their ideal bodies to total strangers. They are insecure and require the affirmation of others to lift their spirits. Their contentment stems from external factors, which might harm your overall health.

Real, happy individuals who lead prosperous, successful lives don't feel the need to brag about how wonderful their lives are to others. They are already aware. They are aware of their blessings, good fortune, happiness, and success in life. They have no one to prove anything to.

Practice loving yourself

As we've already covered, having a pessimistic outlook makes it difficult to achieve your objectives. Give yourself some "me" time when you have free time rather than wasting it on Facebook or other social media. Give yourself a lovely treat. Maybe it's a bubble bath. Maybe just a peaceful cup of tea and a moment to read. Everybody has interests they would want to pursue but put off because they believe their lives are too hectic. Savor a little indulgence without breaking the bank since these modest life objectives inspire creativity and positivity. For instance, you don't have bubble baths since your time is too occupied with the kids. Treat yourself if you have a moment while the children are at school. Savor the bubbly. Set modest but attainable goals for yourself that you can accomplish with a little effort.

You should develop a list of the goals, something akin to a "bucket list," and write them down. Some examples of specific goals are provided below.

Every day, I'll read for thirty minutes.

I'm going to have a massage.

I intend to have a bubble bath.

I'm going to treat myself to some new pants.

I'm going to get dressed up and get coffee with a friend.

These are all straightforward objectives with a clear aim. Setting attainable goals first allows you to gradually increase their difficulty while maintaining their doability. You might not be getting enough exercise, so consider making a point of walking somewhere you would normally drive. Choose easy-to-achieve goals and rejoice that your positive thinking has helped you reach them, no matter how minor they may be. Small goals foster a good mindset that can help you reach larger ones in the future. It's a very beneficial practice because you are educating your mind.

Sixth Insight: Quit Being a Control Addict

You should not allow yourself to become a control freak, even if you must take responsibility for your activities and lead a self-sufficient existence. Although it gives you a sense of control over your life, going too far in the wrong direction can also cause you to feel dissatisfied. So, giving up on control is the sixth tip for achieving true happiness and embracing success in your life.

Give Up and Quit Trying to Control Everything

You begin to believe you are the only one overseeing everything when you take on an incredibly controlling attitude toward every facet of your life. Since this is untrue, when things don't go your way and take an unexpected turn, you get dissatisfied and depressed. The truth is that there are things beyond your control. All you have power over is yourself. You do not influence how other people act or how certain circumstances transpire. It will be advantageous to acknowledge this fact as soon as possible. You may relieve great mental and physical strain when you give up trying to manage and control everyone and everything in your immediate environment. You quit being persistent and whiny, you quit worrying all the time, and you quit taking charge. You feel at ease, content, and joyful as these things shift.

Here's what you need to do to become less bossy and domineering if you truly want to relax and experience happiness rising within you.

Give up nagging

First and foremost, you must stop pestering others so much. Avoid constantly criticizing your loved ones for their mistakes and what they ought to have done. They are aware of their obligations. Simply relax and give them some room to breathe. They will feel less stressed due to your nagging, and they will gradually understand and fulfill their responsibilities.

Limit Your Thoughts to Your Perspective

Give no more of your peace of mind to people you encounter, especially those closest to you. Please stop being so controlling and stop talking about yourself all the time. People don't like it when you constantly dictate what to do. Instead, give it a vacation. By making this adjustment, you'll quickly notice that your loved ones are becoming nicer and warmer to you, and as your connections get better, you begin to feel happier.

Have faith in the universe.

Finally, you must believe in the universe to provide only positive things. If you begin to believe in this advice, you will quickly discover that you are taking advantage of incredible possibilities and that you don't need to alter or take control of your life.

Use these techniques to fill your life with genuine calm and peace.

Seventh insight: Stay optimistic and in the moment

Yes, life might be unpredictable, but if you pay close attention, you'll notice that you have 24 hours a day, just like everyone else. The only thing that separates you from the joyful group is that they actively fill their time with activities. At the same time, you dwell on your regrets, worries about the future, and other unfavorable thoughts. You must begin to be optimistic and live in the present rather than the past or future to draw genuine joy, satisfaction, and abundance into your life.

Staying Positive and Aware of the Here and Now

You'll discover that your thoughts are negative, regretful, and filled with worries if they are mired in the past or the future. You can never get prosperity, abundance, or pleasure if your thoughts are negative. Why? Because for these things to happen, you have to have a positive growth mentality, which can only be accomplished when your mind is clear of negative thoughts. On the other hand, positive thinking gives you the ability to see the good things ahead of you in the present and to believe in the possibilities. As soon as you begin to live in the now and recognize all the benefits that have come your way, you will feel happy.

If this inspires optimism in you, follow these steps.

Create Optimistic Thoughts

Negative ideas can be eliminated most effectively by not giving them any weight. You can allow bad thoughts to exit your mind and return to their natural state when you stop paying attention. Only when you are thinking is when negativity enters your head. You must thus cease doing that. Make a lot of positive thoughts instead of concentrating on negative ones. Some examples of these are: "I am happy," "I am successful," "I attract abundance towards myself easily," "I am a magnet for prosperity and happiness," and "I am fulfilling my goals." Just keep thinking these and many other similar thoughts all the time. You could even repeat them loudly as affirmations every day. You'll notice that you're thinking more positive and fewer negative thoughts in around two weeks. Now is the time to focus on constructive thoughts so that they fill your head with good things. As you naturally grow more positive, it also helps to surround yourself with positive individuals. But later in this book, a little more about this.

Give Thanks for All of Your Blessings and

Simultaneously, you should develop the habit of identifying any three blessings you have received and writing a detailed account of their importance and necessity in your life. You may write about your wife, work, and automobile, for example, on day one; on day two, you could concentrate on your house, electricity, a healthy body, and so forth. Simply continue writing one little page each day. You will understand that you are incredibly fortunate and blessed in seven days. Additionally, you must begin to thank the universe for all of the blessings you have received. When you express gratitude to the universe, better things come your way, and your life becomes everything you want.

Defend Negative Energy

The Impact of Negative Thoughts on Your Mind

Imagine that as you are traveling on the freeway, the vehicle in front of you starts to fishtail rather badly. Do you think he's going to lose control of his car entirely? The issue is that, in addition to not knowing where this car will wind up if it spins out of control, you also have a semi-truck to your left. Right now, you're scared. Utterly terrified.

That terror brings intense attention. How to prevent a disastrous accident is all that's on your mind. Fear is useful in this situation because it forces you to focus. However, fear, rage, and other unfavorable ideas can often be harmful. Why? They are harmful because, although the thought is frequently superfluous, our minds react to it as though it were, as seen in the previously outlined example involving the car accident. In response to these feelings, our minds block out possibilities and the advantages of positive thinking by narrowing our focus to the issue. Negative thinking can focus attention, which is beneficial in an emergency but harmful in other contexts.

The unfortunate paradox is that, as our minds attempt to find a solution, negative ideas make us concentrate even more on the negative. Whenever we think something unpleasant, our mind tries to "avoid the accident." Imagine that tomorrow is the deadline for a significant project at work. When you arrive home to do the project, you discover that your kid was physically assaulted by the school bully and chastised for fighting. You are enraged with both the bully and the school. You control this pessimistic idea and cannot concentrate on the task. You let down other coworkers when you could not concentrate, missed the deadline, and did not finish the project.

Because of the way it affects your mind and blocks out any happy thoughts and the advantages that come with them, negative thinking is harmful.

The Impact of Positive Thoughts on Your Mind

According to the study in this book's introduction, thinking positively broadens our mind, while thinking negatively narrows it. Long-term excellent functioning is produced by positive thinking. Joy inspires play and creative expression. The drive to discover, educate oneself, and take on new experiences is fueled by the pleasant emotion of interest. The desire to relish life's circumstances arises from contentment. Love, which is thought to be a concoction of happy feelings, gives us the desire to explore, play, and enjoy our loved ones.

Positive thoughts can influence a person over time by strengthening their assets, while negative thoughts, when used appropriately, can be beneficial in the here and now. Young people develop motor skills that they will need later in life via play. Additionally, social ties formed by play help people in almost every aspect of life. Every happy feeling improves a person's qualities in some way. They could improve someone's intellectual, psychological, social, or physical well-being. According to the study's findings, the benefits of positive thinking are long-lasting and enduring. In bad times, people can rely on the resources they have acquired through optimistic thinking.

The potential to use positive thinking to undo the harm caused by negative thinking was one of the hypotheses examined during the study. The anxiety-inducing scenario that the researchers placed the research volunteers in caused an increase in heart rate and blood pressure. Following that, they split the subjects up to watch a single movie. The participants watch one of four types of films: one that makes them happy, one that makes them happy or sad. The researchers discovered that although none of the films impacted the cardiovascular system without the anxiety-inducing test, they did impact individuals who had the test. Compared to the control group, which saw a neutral film, those who saw the films for happiness and contentment recovered more quickly from the spike in heart rate and blood pressure. After the anxiety-inducing exam, the people who saw a depressing movie recovered the least quickly out of all the groups.

How to Think More Positively Throughout Your Life

Remember from the last chapter that unpleasant thoughts and feelings serve a function and shouldn't just be discounted or disregarded. Their purpose is to promote growth and healing. Here, addressing the underlying problems that give rise to the pessimistic ideas is crucial. There will not be long-lasting change if the underlying problems are not resolved. After addressing negative thinking, we can consider enhancing our positive thought patterns.

Thinking positively and engaging in our fitness regimen

The Motor Performance and Learning Laboratory at UNLV has researched motivation and optimism during exercise. [i]

Positive encouragement

A person's perception of competence increases when they receive favorable feedback during a workout; in other words, they think they are good at the exercise for which they received positive feedback. Perhaps this explains why the CrossFit community, where participants encourage one another, is so well-liked—positive reinforcement inspires each individual. According to studies, athletes perform at their best and learn the most when they feel confident in their abilities and think they are performing well. Thus, how will this benefit those who lack confidence or experience? The premise is that you should surround yourself with supportive individuals who provide constructive criticism.

Establishing Goals

Do you have any memories of being awarded a prize? I composed a poem when I was nine years old, and it won me a fountain pen. I have carried that good experience with me throughout my entire life. Looking at your life goals, you may easily find moments of happiness like that. Maybe all you want to do today is feel better about life. If so, jot down a list of things you can do to improve your mood in your notepad. These don't even need to be intricate objects. Things like taking a bath, cleaning your hair, and styling it can lift your spirits when you're depressed and not taking care of yourself.

After I list my blessings each morning, I automatically evaluate the day. There's always more work to be done than time available. As a result, worrying about being unable to accomplish everything is pointless. You must set priorities. If I don't iron the clothes, the world won't end. If I cannot complete something that I should have, it won't change. We notice all these bad things in our lives and give them far more weight than they deserve. Make a realistic list of the things you want to do today and write it down. Start modest, as you will regret not accomplishing everything if you overextend yourself. That isn't going to exactly inspire optimism. Consequently, your list should first be achievable, and as you gain confidence, you can add to it to achieve that amazing sense of motivation.

Keep the list with you throughout the day and do each item on it one at a time, marking your progress with a pen that is easy to see. For the first few days, list things you know you can accomplish. Then, push yourself beyond. You'll be surprised by yourself because when you start to see results, it inspires you to work even harder. Your brain enjoys challenges and may be a great ally in assisting you to transition from a negative phase to a positive one.

I'll give you an illustration. You are aware of the neglected relationships in your life. You are also aware of your disregard for your house. You currently have a negative outlook on life. You can include easy items like these on your list:

I'm going to call my mom today.

I'm going to organize the closet today.

I'm going to walk for twenty minutes today.

I'll eat fewer carbohydrates today.

Consider your list, whatever items it may contain, as a tool for constructively managing your life. Overwhelming yourself won't do anything to raise your positivity levels. One thing that needs to be on your daily agenda is making time for yourself. You should include something that improves your well-being since YOU are the most significant character in your life. It can be discarding something you don't like. Taking a bubble bath might be it. Saying "no" to an interested parker who takes advantage of you and depresses you about life could do it. There should be one item about YOU and how much you love life.

Congratulations on finishing your list and using it as a reminder that you can complete the activities you set out to accomplish. Even the most basic jobs can be accomplished straightforwardly; one such method is to just begin working on the subject at hand and keep going until it is finished. Do not allow the outside world to divert you. Turn off your social media accounts. Turn off all outside distractions, focus on the work, and cross it off your list.

You'll discover that individuals often erect obstacles for themselves and prevent themselves from succeeding. They make excuses, and you are done making them. All you need to do is adjust your list to your situation and the difficulty you can handle, and you'll know that you have accomplished your goals.

Section Three

The Advantages of Developing Positive Thoughts

Although there are things in our lives that we cannot control, we can influence our thoughts and reactions. Our mentality will dictate our approach to overcoming any challenges that may arise. And I can assure you that adopting a positive outlook will improve your attitude and make your life happier.

The following are the advantages of developing a positive outlook:

Lower rate of depression, a lower level of distress, increased resistance to colds, improved psychological and physical well-being, and an extended life span, according to the Mayo Clinic.

A higher-quality sleep is an additional advantage of being a cheerful thinker.

Numerous health and mental benefits come from getting enough sleep.

Better stress management: Being positive-thinking does not imply that you have no issues; rather, it indicates that you can deal with stress and recover more quickly while still finding the positive aspects of any given circumstance. Let's take a scenario where your presentation went badly. If you are an optimist, you will devise a plan of action to fix your mistakes rather than moping over your failure since you know there are still opportunities. On the other hand, if you are a pessimist, you will give up easily, see yourself negatively, and believe that there is nothing you can do.

Your defense or coping method to keep yourself from giving in to irritation or depression will be positive thinking.

Improved relationships: Optimistic people are more content with their relationships since they tend to concentrate more on the positive elements of other people.

You will exude bright energy and spread your happiness and upbeat spirit to others since you also have a better disposition. People will want to work for you as a result of this.

Improved abilities: A positive outlook will motivate you to work toward honing your abilities and building up your resources for the future. Optimists think that rather than giving up, they may climb above and become better than they were.

Increased self-esteem: According to psychologists, self-esteem is an individual's total self-worth or self-value. When you think negatively, you also tend to think poorly of yourself. You will often lower yourself and think that you are incapable of handling any stress or worry that comes with dealing with life's problems. On the other hand, it also follows that someone with a good self-image can better evaluate situations, make decisions, work through issues, and generally have a healthier and more fulfilling life.

Increased productivity at work: As CollenBarret once stated, "Work is either enjoyable or tedious." Your attitude will determine this. I appreciate having fun." A positive outlook is the greatest tool for increasing your enjoyment at work and achieving success. Your attitude will shift from handling routine workplace stress, your boss's criticism, or even your demanding coworkers to optimism. Because you have faith in your ability to achieve anything, you will quickly discover that you can work longer hours (without being sidetracked by negative ideas) and even find ways to be more productive. A positive outlook might also put you on the path to success since it will make you more receptive to opportunities. You'll have a positive outlook on work and self-belief. These are essential components of success. You will undoubtedly be promoted if you maintain your positive, can-do attitude.

Mindfulness: Mindfulness is an intangible that money cannot truly purchase. You must remove all negative energy and thoughts and think only good thoughts to do this. Optimistic people can let go of almost all negative ideas, including disappointment, anger, and anxiety. Never forget that happiness and tranquility are not the products of negative thinking. Peace of mind also leads to inner enjoyment, which will undoubtedly come from you.

Positivity makes one feel more motivated, grateful, and inspired to tackle things.

Positive thinking is not the same as seeing the world through rose-colored glasses. This indicates that we are aware of reality and view things more positively. We concentrate on what we can control, including our ideas, feelings, and behaviors, since we know we are not in charge of everything. It's the capacity to turn any circumstance around and overcome whatever challenges life throws at you. Being happy instead of depressed, calm instead of irrational, and smiling bravely instead of shedding tears of defeat are all examples of positive thinking.

Especially when things don't seem to be going our way or achieving our idealized "perfection" seems difficult, there are moments when it seems easier to give up and think negatively. Ultimately, though, ask yourself if that makes you happier. Never forget the great effects that thinking positively may have on you and those around you.

Do not worry if you are a pessimistic thinker but are eager or open to change; the following chapter will assist you in making the shift to becoming an optimist. You're about to become a better version of yourself!

Chapter 6: It's Time To Empty Your Bad Buddy Closet

Eliminating toxic friendships could be the best action if negative people surround you, as Joel Osteen famously stated."

I cut out friendships in my life that were turning into contagious bad habits at this time of transition. Those people made me wonder who I was, and I didn't want to retain them in my life any longer. I had to get as far away as possible from the people who were always talking down to me. Everybody has that one friend who is so toxically infatuated with negativity that they are constantly chatting about their new partner. But you have to eliminate everyone, putting a bad twist in your path because if you don't, those bad influences will keep pulling you back from realizing your goals.

I realized that I had to cut those relationships out of my life, so I began turning my life around. Pessimism "needs a little company to thrive," as the phrase goes, and when that company leaves, pessimism begins to hunt for new possibilities. You need to surround yourself with individuals who share your beliefs if you want to alter your mentality.

A friend of mine informed me a few years ago that she worked at a company where she saw many women similar to the local bad recruiters for the just-hired staff. They would freely plant pessimistic notions about the job and advancement in the minds of some of the more recent hires. Like a gang of cobras, they would tighten their grip on their target once they had it. Many of these women had worked for the company for years, even decades, but they had all persuaded themselves that a promotion was not necessary for them to advance in their careers. It wasn't until one courageous day that a colleague applied for a managerial position since she was eager for a change. She was hired!

This moment altered their consistent path of action and allowed them to recognize a favorable occasion that impacted their own. These women had been letting fear prevent them from getting the one thing they had always wanted—a promotion—for years. Fear can be like a plague that swallows anything if one does not grab a grip and fight back. If you have gone through something similar, I would advise you to cut the bad friendships that keep you from moving on to the next prosperous phase of your life.

The first thing you should do if toxic people surround you is to end those ties. Those living in terror are typically the ones spreading those pessimistic beliefs. As a result, they cast doubt on others in the hopes that they would fail. By ending those relationships, you'll be able to free your mind from the unfavorable ideas that are always bothering you. After that, you'll be free to start your path to optimism.

Always try to be in the company of positive, like-minded individuals. You want folks like these to stand behind your choices and ambitions. These motivating personalities will support and mentor you as you work toward your objectives.

The Ability of Two Easy Techniques to Increase Happiness

There are two rather easy techniques you can use to assist yourself in becoming happier. Although many individuals are aware of these two methods, many seem to downplay their significance in improving their own and other people's moods.

An easy activity to start with is this one. It's excellent if you have a mirror handy! Notice how your face is currently expressing yourself. If you haven't previously, flex your mouth's side muscles now. Now that you've completed this exercise correctly, you should be grinning! Yes, even if you're not joyful or upbeat, the easiest thing you can do is simply grin. Some people may find it difficult at first, but with practice, you can maintain your smile, which will cause others to smile back at you. Additionally, investigations and research have indicated that smiling alone elevates your mood. Thus, maintaining that smile will lift your spirits!

Try the alternative exercise; it may seem easy initially, but most people find it more challenging. This entails being very aware of your thoughts. Throughout the day, you'll probably think adversely about particular individuals, situations, or events that you encounter or react badly in your head. The idea is to prevent yourself from harboring thoughts of this nature. Find a method to ignore unpleasant thoughts as soon as you notice them.

You might try to bargain with yourself, requiring yourself to contribute a quarter to your "be more positive" fund each time you have a negative thought. Alternately, set a goal to think as little negatively as possible during the day. Reframing something that appears bad into something positive may make you feel better about yourself and your capacity to handle difficult situations constructively.

In the next section, you'll discover more about an excellent method for practicing mental relaxation.

Exercise Suggestions: Try to grin a little bit as you wake up. With a mirror in front of you, practice this to increase your feeling of positivity.

Set aside a certain day to focus on noticing any unpleasant ideas that cross your mind. Try your hardest not to say them, to let go of them, and to replace them with more upbeat thoughts. As you establish a new habit, extend this to multiple days in a row.

Strength Of Cleaning Up Your Social Media

Depending on how you use them, social media platforms like Facebook, Instagram, Twitter, and others can be entertaining but sometimes have drawbacks. You studied how to start your day with a good outlook and prevent negative ideas from entering your mind in the previous part. You may ensure that you accomplish that by surrounding yourself with good individuals or organizations, but managing your social media accounts is also important.

Facebook can be the biggest offender for certain folks. Although it's a fantastic tool for staying in touch with loved ones, you follow certain users who often criticize or publish divisive content. The best course of action is to "unfollow" them or select "Hide this post" or "Hide all from" by clicking the arrow or menu on their post. You can start limiting how many unfavorable posts you see.

This will be a very difficult job for many individuals, even while it is probably easy to recognize folks who are unpleasant on social media or who negatively influence us. We typically wish to be updated about our close friends and family members. The advantages of staying home, though, can be offset by the possibility that every time we see their messages on social media, they negatively influence us. Whether your associations are on Facebook, Twitter, Instagram, or any other social media platform you use frequently, review them thoroughly.

You may keep up with multiple fan pages or websites sharing popular news or celebrity rumors. It might be time to unfriend those Facebook pages if you notice that they frequently post depressing content with many angry comments.

You can clear your mind of constrictive and negative thoughts by purging your social media contacts or not utilizing social media as often as others. Put this method into practice as soon as possible.

Exercise Suggestion: Allocate a specific period to examine your social media profiles, paying close attention to the ones you may utilize most frequently. Look for posts from people or pages you follow that seem generally depressing. If so, you might want to unfollow them or hide their posts from your timeline.

The Fifth Chapter: Who Are You?

Now that you have a better understanding of happiness and its various forms, it's time to assess yourself to understand who you are. Are you able to be joyful because you love yourself enough? These are a few self-help questions you can ask yourself and some guidance on assessing your responses.

Are you content right now?

Are you happy with the current state of your life? Do you feel content with your life, family, and work? If the response is affirmative, you may be content now. This question helps you assess your level of happiness, allowing you to continue doing the things that bring you joy and, if you discover you are not, to identify the things that bring you sorrow. In this sense, you can either quit doing the things that bring you down or remain joyful.

What brings you joy? What are those things?

After determining whether or not you are happy, you need to ascertain what brings you happiness. You must compare them to what you are already doing as soon as you discover them. You are performing well if it appears that you are already doing them. If you've discovered that you're unhappy despite appearing to be doing what makes you happy, you need to assess whether these activities truly bring you happiness; if not, you must look for other sources of happiness.

Do you feel at ease?

It's time to ask yourself if you're content with the direction your life is currently taking now that you know what brings you happiness. Do you believe that you are on the correct track and that the next day's events don't concern you? You are truly at ease if your response is in the affirmative.

Do you feel pain?

You might want to reconsider if you don't seem at ease. Are there any obstacles preventing you from experiencing inner peace? What specific items are causing you to feel this way? Work them out so you can analyze them and determine how to handle them.

Are you prepared to decide on the type of happiness you truly desire?

You now clearly understand who you truly are, how you're feeling, and why it's time to decide the kind of happiness you want to seek. If you know you'll be happy, do you believe you can handle some significant changes in your life? If so, you can move on to choosing the kind of happiness you wish to seek.

It's time to learn how to go after your intended result now that you have assessed yourself and know your true feelings and emotional state. How can you seek out and, with minimal difficulty, obtain true happiness? Here are a few things to consider if you want to be genuinely happy.

Acceptance and Moving Forward with the Now

To truly pursue happiness, you must first realize that you must be able to accept who you are, what you have done, and your past. Despite the negative things that occurred in the past, you have to accept the past fully. Keep your attention on the now and now, and remember that accepting life's challenges can help you find true pleasure. Remember that you can still do many things in life as long as you acknowledge that you are in the present.

Every man is sinful.

This is the stage of the journey where you must acknowledge that you are a human being and that you will occasionally make mistakes that the other people watching you may see as sins. Recognize that this is typical and that similar events will inevitably occur. There will be times when you give in to temptation since it is always present. The key to success is ensuring you can make the correct decision more often. You must try to keep temptation out of your heart and your door.

Whatever gets done gets done.

You cannot undo the things that have already happened to you; they will always have the same effect on your present. You cannot change the things that have already been done. You can alter the course of events by making sure you never make the same mistakes twice and by giving everything you do your all. By pursuing your passions and making the most of your free time, you may constantly strive to live a better life. All you need to do is play the appropriate cards; the rest is up to you.

Confession, learning to let go, and relieving oneself of any guilt or emotional load

The fact that finding happiness is a process is a plus. At least, it is not how true happiness works; you do not get joyful immediately. Furthermore, since it's a process, you can take things slowly to preserve your sanity. Admit that you are to blame for these issues and express regret for your mistakes. Give up on the things that are hurting and causing you discomfort. You will be able to live a better and happier life after you release yourself from any mental load and guilt you may have. Take it easy and allow yourself to be freed from emotional tension. Don't allow the things that have already happened to ruin your life. Knowing when to let go and when to hang on is a necessary skill.

The secret is to get better every day.

Doing nice deeds may assist you in releasing yourself from the things that are causing you pain or distress. You'll find that life is much easier if you master the art of selflessness. Certain things are only accessible to you when you carry out nice deeds. Give your heart permission to express itself. Helping others and being kind and generous will pay off handsomely, as you will see when you get the thank-yous from the individuals you've helped and witness the smiles on their cheeks. Your dreams will be significantly better than ever, and you can sleep through the night more easily.

adherence to and application of the Universal Laws

The rules governing Zen happiness are something known as universal laws. They are your road map to obtaining happiness that endures for a considerable amount of time, if not forever. It is important to strive to live by these laws, believe in them, and apply them to your everyday existence. Among these laws are the laws of attraction, giving, and Karma, among many more. You will learn more about these laws and hear a detailed discussion of them in the upcoming chapter. You merely need to understand what they are for the time being. The law of giving then tells you to give to other people to be happier since, as you may know, Karma is a force that returns what you have given to others.

The Law of Attraction and Hope

Happiness is undoubtedly correlated with optimism. You can see the hidden beauty that others miss because they are too lazy to look for it when you choose to always see the bright side of things. Living an optimistic life is essential as it reduces depression and increases happiness. You can improve your relationships with other people by trying not to think badly of them. Conversely, applying the law of attraction is similar to drawing in what you desire by engaging in related activities. The following chapters will cover this topic in more detail.

You've learned a few things in this chapter that you can do to start living the happy life you truly want. It is up to you to decide how to apply these principles to your life to find happiness. Ultimately, you are ultimately responsible for your happiness since only you can choose to live a happier life. What to do after you've finally grasped the bliss you've always craved is covered in the next chapter.

Exercise Frequently

Regular exercise has been shown in studies to enhance memory recall. By boosting the production of hormones linked to memory development and consolidation, it enhances both your spatial memory and general cognitive function. Furthermore, exercise boosts your brain's grey matter, which enhances your memory and recall of knowledge.

Any physical activity will do; try to walk for ten minutes each day, practice yoga or aerobics, swim, play a sport, or merely dance. The key is to perform anything strenuous for a while to get the health advantages of exercise. To maximize the benefits of the practice, extend its length throughout time. Establish a schedule. Following a set pattern can assist you in generating conscious thought and, ultimately, taking action.

Make mental maps

Mind maps are excellent visual aids for improving concentration, sparking creative thoughts, and helping you recall information quickly to make wise judgments. This is how one can be made:

Jot down the main idea—a fact, a choice, an issue, or anything else you wish to commit to memory or practice. You could doodle something about it, upload an image, or write a quote.

Next to the main idea, draw branches, then label the branches with pertinent words, pictures, and doodles. The main concepts associated with the main notion comprise the branches. The branches will list the various marketing approaches you can use, for example, if you are developing a marketing strategy for your product.

Draw as many sub-branches under a main branch as you like, as branches can contain sub-branches that define and explain concepts and strategies for putting those ideas into practice.

When you're finished, repeat the mind map several times to help you remember it.

Using these tactics will ensure that you take action. This approach, along with all the others, assists you in making decisions that enhance your life.

Getting Rid Of Fear And Doubt

Fear and doubt are two of the largest things that might prevent you from reaching your goals and leading a happy life. They can impair your judgment, erode your self-assurance, and make you lose focus on your objectives. But it's crucial to understand how to get past these unfavorable feelings and ideas if you want to use the Law of Attraction and the power of positive thought.

Recognizing the source of your anxiety and doubt is one of the first steps toward conquering them. Sometimes, because of bad conditioning or experiences from the past, they could be firmly embedded in your subconscious. In other instances, they might be the outcome of the current situation, like a lack of resources or other people's viewpoints.

The secret to conquering fear and doubt is recognizing them and then taking action to deal with them, regardless of their origin. This could entail confronting unfavorable thoughts or self-talk, asking for help from others, or taking proactive steps to face your anxieties and move on.

Using visual aids to help you overcome doubt and fear is quite effective. Focus on good outcomes rather than negative ones by imagining yourself reaching your goals and leading a happy life. You can use this to change your perspective and overcome any limiting thoughts preventing you from moving forward.

Affirmations are another powerful tool for conquering doubt and anxiety. You can start to reprogram your brain to focus on happy ideas and feelings by telling yourself positive affirmations daily. Your self-worth and confidence may increase, motivating you toward your objectives.

When overcoming fear and doubt, engaging in self-care and self-compassion exercises is critical. This is treating yourself with kindness, accepting that mistakes will be made, and realizing that obstacles are a normal part of the journey. Taking care of yourself may strengthen your inner power and resilience, enabling you to face and conquer any obstacles.

Ultimately, keeping your attention in the here and now is critical rather than becoming bogged down in thinking about the future or living in the past. You can start to let go of fear and doubt and concentrate on the wonderful opportunities and experiences currently accessible by developing your present mindfulness.

Living a positive and fulfilling life requires overcoming fear and doubt, which can be difficult. You may start using positive thinking and the Law of Attraction to reach your objectives and lead the life you desire by learning to recognize and deal with these unfavorable feelings and ideas.

Examining Various Motivational Methods

It is essential to find inner inspiration throughout difficult times and to never give up. This chapter explores the several motivating strategies that can stoke our inner fire and enable us to go beyond any roadblock in our achievement. This chapter will provide the tools to kickstart your motivation and rekindle your passion for life, regardless of whether you are dealing with personal or professional setbacks or feeling uninspired.

The concept of motivation is not universally applicable. What motivates one individual might not be suitable for another. Experimenting with several approaches is crucial to determine which ones work best for you and your objectives. This section provides a thorough overview of various motivational tactics so you may identify which ones will be most helpful to you on your path to success.

The power of goal setting is one strategy that is covered. A successful plan can be made by establishing specific and attainable goals. The SMART goal-setting framework (Specific, Measurable, Attainable, Relevant, Time-bound) is examined in this subchapter, along with helpful advice on creating objectives that will inspire you and help you stay on course.

Another strategy investigated is the use of visualization and the power of positive affirmations. You may rewire your mind to believe in your skills and draw success by telling yourself positive affirmations and visualizing your desired results. Detailed instructions on integrating visualization and positive affirmations into your everyday practice are given in this subchapter.

This chapter also explores the significance of self-motivation and self-care. You can cultivate your motivation from within by learning about methods like seeking support from loved ones, exercising regularly, and practicing mindfulness.

This subchapter concludes by examining the value of associating yourself with like-minded people and looking for accomplished role models for inspiration. You can increase your motivation by surrounding yourself with uplifting and inspiring people and getting knowledge from individuals who have conquered similar obstacles.

To summarize, "Exploring Different Motivational Techniques" offers a thorough manual for locating the drive required to overcome obstacles and succeed. By realizing the effectiveness of goal-setting, self-care, positive affirmations, and seeking inspiration from others, you may stoke your inner fire and persevere through the most trying circumstances. This subchapter gives you the tools to find the methods that work for you so that you may overcome any setback and reach your full potential.

Chapter 7: Overcoming Self-Doubt and Procrastination

Knowledge of Procrastination and Its Effects

Many people experience the frequent phenomena of procrastination, particularly during difficult circumstances. It is the practice of putting off or postponing work, frequently leading to lower output and higher stress levels. In "Fueling the Fire Within Discovering

Motivation for Success," we examine the subtleties of procrastination and its significant effects on our lives.

Understanding procrastination is essential for those who need to find motivation to persevere through difficult situations. It is a barrier that can impede development and keep people from reaching their objectives.

A major roadblock in our quest for success in life is procrastination. It is frequently rooted in perfectionism, fear of failing, or a vague sense of what we want to achieve. We delay taking action and let self-doubt sneak in when we procrastinate, eventually hindering our growth. We must first recognize these tendencies and comprehend their effect on our motivation to break away from the procrastination cycle.

Furthermore, motivation for overcoming obstacles and hardship becomes even more crucial when faced with challenging situations. Procrastination can make These difficulties worse, making people feel helpless and overwhelmed. Examining the underlying causes of procrastination, we can pinpoint tactics for regaining drive and overcoming hardship.

Procrastination also affects areas outside of our personal lives. Strained relationships with coworkers on the job. By being aware of the negative effects of procrastination, we can actively resist it and create a more positive and productive work atmosphere.

This chapter delves into the psychology of procrastination, examining the causes of our actions and how they affect our drive and achievement. In addition, we will offer useful advice and methods for overcoming procrastination, rekindling our drive, and succeeding in life despite obstacles we might encounter.

By comprehending the complexities of procrastination and its effects, we may arm ourselves with the resources required to surmount this barrier and pursue achievement. When motivation keeps us going, we may overcome obstacles, accomplish our objectives, and persevere through hardship.

Section Three

The Strength of Positive Thought

If you harness the power of positive thought, you can achieve all you have ever desired. One thing that the most successful individuals in the world would agree on if you asked them to share the keys to their success is that they have a positive outlook, never give up, and have faith in their ability to succeed. In action, this is optimistic thinking.

By helping you to stay focused on your objectives, positive thinking can help you modify your mindset and strategy for pursuing your goals. You'll discover that, with little to no effort, things in your life seem to go in your favor. One important law controls this. The attraction legislation.

The Attraction Law

According to the law of attraction, like attracts like. It also demonstrates that you are in charge of all circumstances in your life, whether favorable or unfavorable, due to your thoughts. As a result, your ideas caused you to be late for a meeting since you were caught in traffic. Your thoughts led to the conditions if you experienced a difficult breakup in which you felt deceived or mistreated. Your ideas cause any lucky spells you experience when things seem to go your way.

When positive things happen in your life, you will readily acknowledge that your mind is fully in charge of these situations and thoughts; nevertheless, when bad things happen, you may feel like you have no control over anything. This is untrue since everything—

good and bad—is under your control. All of it is in your head.

You may use the law of attraction to make your thoughts come true and attract tangible objects and events into your life. In light of this, you must think positively in whatever situation you may find yourself to draw positive energy and favorable outcomes. This is a perfect example of "seeing the bright side of life."

This is an actual instance. When you arrive at work, you discover that everything you own—including computers and paper records—has been destroyed by a terrible accident and fire. The projects you have been working on are gone, and with them, all the customer information you needed to do your job properly. To catch up, there are a lot of things that need to be done. Consider this situation a possibility rather than crashing to your knees theatrically, raising your hands, and yelling, "Why?" Firstly, you might have lost your life in the fire, so be grateful that you were not at work. Fortunately, your clients' phone numbers are saved on your cell phone, so you can begin retrieving all of your data immediately. In addition, you can get information from your email, and most of your data is cloud-stored. You will receive the necessary funds to reestablish; given your insurance, things might work out better this time. By shifting your negative thinking to positive ones, you will draw good things to yourself and improve your circumstances.

Using Positive Thoughts to Your Advantage

You always hear a voice in your brain asking you questions about the decisions you are making, making you wonder if they are the right ones. This voice also leads to negative thinking by persuading you that you are powerless, that things are not going your way, and that the situation is worse than it seems. You can turn off this voice by directing your attention to your attitude and thoughts. This is the method: -

Encouragement Phrases

Saying affirmations to yourself is an effective way to influence both your conscious and subconscious minds positively. When you recite these affirmations, you are meant to feel inspired, driven, and completely invigorated. When you repeat a positive affirmation, your subconscious mind can image what you are saying, which helps you stay in a positive state of mind and controls your behavior, particularly your habits and actions.

You will discover that utilizing a positive affirmation can help you focus on your objective and change the world from the inside out as you strive to harness the power of positive thinking.

If you want to employ positive affirmations to your advantage, how you apply them matters. Though you can choose to repeat your affirmations throughout the day, it is preferable to say your positive affirmations first thing in the morning. Remember to focus on the desired outcome and speak your affirmation passionately so you may truly feel and believe what you're saying.

You can use the following affirmations in your daily life: -

All facets of my life are prosperous.

I always seem to find happiness.

My health is improving steadily every day.

I attract money, and it finds its way into my life.

My friends and family are overflowing with affection for me.

The more you repeat these affirmations and give them credence, the quicker positivity can enter your day-to-day existence.

Component 2 of Small Thinking: Passivity

Being passive is the antithesis of being active. For instance, a man and his wife argue about who should go lock the door in the amusing poem Get Up and Bar the Door. They conclude in the poem that the person who speaks first ought to lock the door. As the poem progresses, two robbers enter the house and consume the man and wife's food. The irony is that while the husband and wife observe the thieves, they remain silent since they don't want to deal with closing the door.

This embodies passivity perfectly. When someone observes something that has to be done but does nothing about it, they are in the passive spirit. Small thinkers are mainly inactive because it is far simpler to be passive than to lead an active life.

It's difficult to act. When you take action to accomplish something, you may encounter opposition, difficulty, and pain. You may also have challenges to overcome. But ultimately, leading an active life leads to goal achievement.

As a result, living a passive existence seems easier. Feels is the essential word here. You get instant satisfaction, a sense of relaxation, and relief from the pressure of making decisions when you choose to do nothing. While choosing the less difficult route initially results in less emotional upheaval, this doesn't last very long.

A passive existence is one in which you don't wake up every day trying to maximize your time, money, and energy, or you would prefer to let someone else make the decisions for you. Many people lead inactive lives without recognizing it; they do not realize that doing nothing is still a choice.

Passivity eventually leads to activities one doesn't want to accomplish, occupations one doesn't want, degrees that don't align with one's life goals, and, in certain situations, even marriages one wasn't truly in love with. One of Thinking Big's worst adversaries is passivity! Passivity manifests as:

Postponing a crucial choice till later

- Failing to do important daily chores

- Not devoting enough time and energy to planning
- Not putting in place items like a savings plan or budget that call for discipline
- Postponing taking action until a certain occasion, such as waiting until the first of the year to begin an exercise regimen or until you land a better-paying job before beginning to save money.

Component 3 of Small Thinking: Excuses

You are accustomed to making excuses if you frequently say, "Well, I would if it hadn't been for," or "I'm just not smart/strong/clever/educated enough." Excuses are problematic because, with enough effort on your part, you can maintain them. A tiny thinker considers possible obstacles or why they were halted to justify not taking on the problem. A person who makes excuses all the time is blind to the broad picture and most definitely blind to the incredible chances that are there in front of them.

There are good reasons you can't accomplish anything; for instance, you probably won't be able to play an NFL linebacker at age 68. However, we sometimes mistake good reasons for poor ones.

A justification

- Provides an excuse for a personal defect, fault, or inability to handle a circumstance

Does not result in a shift in character

- Just describes why there weren't any answers; doesn't offer any

Assigns blame to something or someone else

Component 4 of Small Thinking: Entitlement

Mark Twain says, "Don't say the world owes you a living, the world owes you nothing, it was here first." Similarly, when we believe that we are above particular jobs or that some activities aren't worth our time, we act in an entitled manner.

The misconception that you have intrinsic worth just by being you is known as entitlement. The brutal truth is that, except for what you are prepared to give, you are worthless to the world. Put another way, you don't deserve anything if you haven't worked for something.

But an entitled individual could believe they are due something simply for turning up. It is much harder to work in reality when one has an entitlement mentality. After spending $40,000 on her degree, a recent college graduate may decline employment offers until her degree is redeemed. She may need to wait years to find one of these jobs. A man may discover that his girlfriend is extremely unhappy with his demands if he believes she "owes" him affection.

The little mind becomes envious in every way; it convinces them they don't need to put in a lot of effort, that they are entitled to something, or, worse, that they can do anything they want and still get excellent results.

An entitlement may manifest as:

- The conviction that one's efforts warrant a certain reward

Refusing to perform some tasks because you believe them to be beneath you

When a free resource disappears, you become irate.

- When thinking about a prospect, you analyze what's in it.

Component 5 of Small Thinking: Absence of Vision

The greatest definition of vision is the ability to establish a significant objective or dream and put in the effort to realize it. A small-minded person doesn't consider the wider picture, objectives, or the steps required to get them. Instead, they could become only daydreaming about what is ahead. How can one distinguish between a vision and a dream? One word: application.

Creating a workable strategy or action plan to carry out a vision is called implementation. Creating a plan to earn enough money to retire is a vision; dreaming of having enough money to retire is merely wishful thinking.

People with narrow minds seldom see beyond their aspirations. They may believe, "I want to be the CEO!" or "I want to buy a house," but they omit the vital step of creating a compelling enough vision to guide them there. Some stay where they are in life due to a lack of vision. Creating a vision is the most important step toward realizing your aspirations and developing your ability to Think Big.

Symptoms of poor vision can include:

Desiring to accomplish a task yet lacking a strategy

An unmistakable desire for something without the willingness to strive for it

- No plans, either long-term or short-term
- Dreams of success devoid of labor
- Entering sweepstakes, lotteries, or schemes to get rich quickly with the expectation that good fortune will grant your wishes.

Component 6 of Small Thinking: Absence of Accountability

This, the lack of accountability, is the most fundamental aspect of little thinking we have covered thus far. One of the key components of Thinking Big is responsibility, as you'll discover in the next chapter. A person incapable of accepting accountability for their mistakes will never grow from them. People cannot take control of their lives and lead according to their terms if they feel that others are always to blame for their flaws. Put another way, you will never improve your situation in life if you do not accept accountability for the decisions and deeds you commit to.

Among the telltale signs of a lack of duty are:

- Other people are constantly to blame for failures

It's simple to place blame on other people.

- Not accepting responsibility for errors, shortcomings, and missteps
- Not taking the initiative to complete a task or endeavor
- Thinking that someone else determines whether you succeed or fail

These six aspects of small thinking reveal the effects of a life driven by ignorance, annoyance, and tiredness. The good news is that you may choose not to lead a life as a shallow thinker if you want! If any of the items on this list resonate with you or if you experience difficulties in any of the areas above, please don't give up! You know how, and you can begin Thinking Big right now. by accepting accountability for all your flaws and mistakes throughout your life! Though it's a major step, remember that we're thinking big! Now, let's go on to the following chapter.

A Chancer To Success Versus Conscious Thoughts

I'm sure you already realize how important it is to think positively and how it might improve your life. Positive thinking does have the benefit of putting you on the correct path, but you still need to work hard to make your journey meaningful. It's true that the harder you work, the luckier you get since nothing in life happens by accident. To excel in your chosen sport, you must practice a great deal, and obtaining high grades requires reading a great deal. These are the fundamental lessons of life.

Nothing would be worthwhile if all it involved was waiting for things to manifest as you sit down. Real achievement requires sweat, and it's precisely this that adds interest to life. Many individuals read about positive thinking and think that's where it ends. Today, I want to educate you and reassure you that change occurs when you act. Start your path to greatness by deciding what you want, having faith in your capacity to succeed, and—above all—putting in the effort to make it happen.

Positive thinking is beneficial because it fosters a progressive mindset by instilling tenacity and self-belief. You'll be sure you are the person you want to be and will do everything you can to make that happen. Work will become pleasurable and less of a chore once you are in the right frame of mind. It's been stated that the mind is so strong that it can make people successful or unsuccessful. We say that you become what you think about because you are more likely to follow a favorable path when you think favorably.

Putting forth more effort and working hard means entering the world and making your opportunities. Instead of waiting for the world to come through for you, help it do so! Keep an open mind in everything you do, and when things don't go your way, be the kind of person who seeks out answers rather than giving up. Improving oneself could mean learning new things and gaining a great deal of experience.

The law of "cause and effect" states that everything you do has an impact, and nothing happens by accident. According to this theory, everything we say, think and do generates waves of energy that go across the universe and produce effects that may or may not be desired. Thus, it is believed that having positive thoughts and deeds is necessary for living a wonderful and better life.

Everything in your thoughts and deeds should reflect your desire for achievement. I'm trying to suggest that if you want to live a happy and prosperous life, you must first think it is possible and then make efforts to make it happen. The concept of "cause and effect" shows you that there's more to life than just thinking positively and that you need to put in a lot more effort to accomplish your objectives.

APPLY STEVE JOBS' MANUAL

You've probably heard of Steve Jobs and aspire to emulate him in several ways. I say this because, besides his money, he gave me an idea that has long since become ingrained in my mind. For many, his life and the narrative he wrote are a constant source of inspiration. His accomplishments are so many that I feel they merit acknowledgment as I work to instill in you the value of hard work and optimistic thinking. So tell me, in detail, how you know him.

The most inventive businessman, Steve Jobs, is credited with revolutionizing several industries, including computing, telephone, and retail. He was the driving force behind Apple Inc. It is well known that his increased focus and determination on his goals allowed him to succeed. He faced many obstacles and difficulties to accomplish his notable accomplishments but never wavered from his main objectives.

Examining his career and achievements closely reveals that Steve Jobs possesses special traits that, if widely embraced, would change the world. His life appears filled with difficulties, but he overcame them all to create a wonderful and fulfilling life. These include the fact that he was adopted after birth, that he struggled mightily to make ends meet while attending classes informally, that his GPA was extremely poor, that he never liked the structure of schools, and so on.

I'm attempting to make the point that you should pursue your life goals if you believe they are something you must do. Don't let your thoughts or situation stop you from making the initial move. As I've already stated, you must truly struggle—or rather, work extraordinarily hard to advance in life. A great deal would not have been produced in Steve Jobs' name if he had not looked past himself and attempted to establish himself. Nothing should stop you from acting on your mission or what you believe is right for you after you've identified it. Steve Jobs' life is worthy of recognition due to his remarkable accomplishments, which have positively impacted the lives of numerous individuals.

www.ingramcontent.com/pod-product-compliance
Lightning Source LLC
Chambersburg PA
CBHW052154110526
44591CB00012B/1964